JOIN CASH FLOW CLUB

We share strategies and practical tips that business owners and entrepreneurs can implement immediately to improve the overall cash flow in their business.

We will talk about inbound cash flow, outbound cash flow, and managing cash flows overall.

Our primary focus is to generate additional revenues and reduce overall expenses, leaving more cash in your business to fund your life goals.

We share the advice that our top experts have field tested over decades as advisors to large and small businesses (and everything in between). Put our collective wisdom to work in your business today!

Scan the QR Code or go directly to our website here:

https://www.globalwellnesshq.com/cash-flow-club

Cash Flow Club Playbook

The Underground Playbook for Business Success

Jeff Borschowa

LEGAL AND CREDITS

DISCLAIMER

This playbook contains the opinions and ideas of the authors and editor. The purpose of this playbook is to provide you with helpful information as you embark on your personal financial wellness journey.

This playbook should not be relied upon solely to make decisions about financial wellness. Careful attention has been paid to ensure the accuracy of the information, but the authors cannot assume responsibility for the validity or consequences of its use. This information is not intended to be all things to all people. Consult with your own financial experts before you take any actions recommended herein.

CREDITS

Editor: Jeff Borschowa

Design, Photos & Layout: Jeff Borschowa | Canva

Pharos Business Services Inc.

To subscribe to the Cash Flow Club Playbook or join our group, please visit:

https://www.globalwellnesshq.com/cash-flow-club

For queries on how to have your article featured in Cash Flow Club, please join our LinkedIn Group at https://www.linkedin.com/groups/14116388.

This book is dedicated to the courageous business owners and entrepreneurs who brave the uncertainties of the world of business every day. Your courage and commitment to living a life on your terms to create your own freedom, money, and impact is inspirational.

To your success!

INSIDE THIS PLAYBOOK

PART 1: WELCOME

NOTES

FOREWORD

Cash flow is a hot topic in business!

There is a commonly shared statistic that eighty percent of small businesses fail in their first five years. Sadly, of those who survive the first five years, another eighty percent fail in the next five years. That means that business overall has about a four percent success rate over a ten-year period. I am sorry, but in what other area of life would we accept a four percent success rate as good?

As a society, we can and must do better. I believe that some of the blame belongs to accountants. I am a recovering accountant, so I can say this. We have the training and tools to help our clients with cash flow. But, we are taught to focus on scorekeeping and compliance, not proactive advice.

You see, accountants have learned that they are less likely to get sued by a client over historical work. It is pretty cut and dried, whether the work was done correctly or not. However, future oriented work and advisory services that help keep businesses alive and thriving are seen as being full of risk.

The advice we give today could full well be proven to be wrong tomorrow. If we stick to score keeping and don't try to predict the future, we are much more likely to be correct.

I urge those who are reading this publication to use it as a starting point for a conversation with your accounting professionals. I also urge you to consider changing professionals if you cannot convince them to help you with managing your cash flow with intention.

Oftentimes, it is not the advice we receive, but the advice we don't receive, that can harm our businesses.

MY PROMISE TO YOU

If you are still with me, I promise not to waste your time. Quite the contrary, I truly hope this playbook gives you options and inspiration when it comes to building a thriving business.

We will be updating this playbook on a regular basis. We welcome your feedback so that we can create a valuable resource for the business networking community.

BEFORE YOU BEGIN READING THIS PLAYBOOK...

Your results from implementing the strategies in the "Cash Flow Club Playbook: The Underground Playbook for Business Success" will only be as good as how well you implement.

Do NOT take any action in this book without discussing your specific business needs with a qualified professional. If you cannot find one, reach out to us via our LinkedIn Group and we will help you find one.

https://www.linkedin.com/groups/14116388

Fair warning, your existing advisors will likely tell you to play it safe or to avoid taking action. That is rarely the best strategy in a fast-moving world.

Seek the advice you need and implement with extreme action if you want to survive and thrive!

To your success!
Jeff Borschowa
https://www.linkedin.com/in/jeff-borschowa

PS I guarantee that you will find at least one or two typos in this publication. They are my gift to you and I hope it gives you a chance to feel superior to me. :-)

A PRIVATE LETTER TO ACCOUNTANTS

Business owners, entrepreneurs, and organizational leaders, please skip over this page. It is a private letter from me to accountants.

Accountants, I know it is not your fault. The world has trained you to be very cautious about offering cash flow advice. Maybe you don't know how to start the conversation with a client about cash flow.

My biggest advice to you is that you need to get comfortable being uncomfortable. The world needs your unique perspective on cash flow, and it needs it now!

Find ways to be comfortable with talking about what will be instead of what was.

There are many great tools out there to help you as you manage cash flow for your clients.

More importantly, your clients will appreciate you more for helping them with real challenges.

Don't know where to start? Read through this guide and share your favorite ideas with your clients.

I believe that you have a moral obligation to help your clients thrive. The days of just surviving are behind us.

We are a community of Cash Flow experts, and we are here to support you as you support your clients. You will literally be saving lives and communities!

Please join us, there is nothing to lose by learning more about Cash Flow!

We are stronger together!

Jeff Borschowa
https://www.linkedin.com/in/jeff-borschowa

INTRODUCTION

Welcome business owners and advisors!

I wrote this book to help you find the resources you need to build a thriving business with consistent, reliable, and predictable cash flows. I wanted to share some of the secrets I have learned in my career as an accountant and an entrepreneur.

It is very important for me to share up front that I do not believe that this playbook will be all things to all people. Every business is unique and every entrepreneur will need their own guidance.

I will be sharing my insights, ideas, ideals, and resources with you. My goal is to uncover the best of the best resources related to building a thriving business through cash flow management..

My hope is that this book will be your guide to building a thriving business that will serve you, your family, and your community.

I will share my philosophy in this book and some strategies you can implement on your own. You can reach out to me if you like my philosophy. And I am perfectly fine if you choose to work on building your thriving business on your own.

You can reach out to me directly at any time if you want more guidance based on what I am sharing with you in this book. The first step in working with me is to join one of our Open Coffee sessions on Zoom.

If we both agree that we might be a good fit to work together, the next step is to schedule a Strategy Session. The goal of the Strategy Session is very simple – to determine if we are a mutual fit to work together. You can reach out to me at any time to schedule a Strategy Session.

We will cover a few things in this book:

- Sharing my cash flow philosophy.
- Exploring the mindset necessary to enhance your cash flow management skills.
- Exploring the skill set necessary to improve your cash flow management skills.
- How to have a deeper impact in your community with a thriving business.
- How to manage your business cash flow by working smarter, not harder.

I want to keep this book short and to the point. I have designed it as a workbook so that you can make notes as you go.

Jeff Borschowa

https://www.linkedin.com/in/jeff-borschowa

WHO SHOULD READ THIS BOOK?

I wrote this book for business owners, entrepreneurs, and professional advisors who want to get better at managing cash flow in business.

You should read this book if:

- You are in some way responsible for adding revenues to a business.
- You are in some way responsible for reducing expenses in a business.
- You are responsible for managing the bottom line cash position of a business.
- You want to manage your cash flow by working smarter, not harder.
- You believe that a thriving business is a great path to making the world a better place.

I will share my best advice on how to build a thriving business by managing your cash flows with intention. I will also be sharing resources to guide you on your journey to improve your mindset, skill set, and gear set.

Whether we work together or not, I encourage you to take the time to read this book and see if there are any strategies that can have a positive impact on your business or life right now.

I have intentionally left many blank pages for you to use to take notes as you cultivate your thriving business.

Feel free to jump to whichever sections of this book appeal to you most. There is no one right way to read this book.

What part of this resonates with you? Why do you want to continue reading this book?

How important is it to you start building a thriving business? Why?

DO I NEED HELP WITH MY CASH FLOW?

We offer this simple diagnostic to help you determine whether you want to initiate a Cash Flow Management Project with our team or on your own to build a thriving business. These statements should guide your decision and give you clarity.

You probably do not need our help if you answer yes to most of these statements. However, if you answered no or maybe, you probably need our help. Even if you answered yes to every question, you may wish to have our team put you on the fast-track to your Cash Flow Management Project.

Question	Yes	Maybe	No
I know with certainty how to increase my inbound cash flows.			
I know with certainty how to accelerate my inbound cash.			
I know with certainty how to systemize my inbound cash flows.			
I know with certainty how to decrease my outbound cash flows.			
I know with certainty how to decelerate my outbound cash.			
I know with certainty how to optimize my outbound cash.			
I know with certainty how to manage my savings.			
I know with certainty how to manage my borrowing.			
I know with certainty how to manage my investing.			

What questions do you have for yourself as you go through this initial diagnostic?

PART 2: THRIVING BUSINESS MODEL

NOTES

CASH FLOW IN A THRIVING BUSINESS

Cash flow problems are the silent killer of many businesses. In my foreword, I shared the statistic that only four percent of businesses survive through their first ten years in business.

That statistic makes my blood boil, it literally pisses me off to no end.

Why? Great question. I have seen first-hand the devastation that a failing business can have. It is not just another empty store front on main street.

I have seen business failures cause so many terrible things to both the owners and employees:

- Families break up due to financial stress.
- Families end up homeless.
- Children are separated from parents.
- Parents work multiple jobs to pay bills.
- Entrepreneurs end up buried in debt.
- Bankruptcy is often the only option for owners.
- Suicide is a staggering choice for some who can't face the prospect of a failed business.

The concept of "losing everything" is very real for those brave entrepreneurs who put their livelihoods on the line.

What can you expect in the Cash Flow Club Playbook? Why is it the underground playbook for business success?

I will share a lot of tips on how you can manage your cash flow today and into the future so that you can prevent "worst case scenarios" and so that you can live your dreams.

Whether you actively manage the cash flow in your business or not, it is actively managing you. Cash flow crunches and shortages will limit the options you have available to your business. Cash flow surpluses (imagine that) will help you scale and grow in ways you might not be able to imagine today.

This playbook is a labor of love from me to you. Consider it my gift to you as you wade through the complexities of up and down markets.

These strategies are time tested and have been proven in every economic situation imaginable.

I do not wish to profit from this playbook. Use it as you see fit. And, when something works for you, please share this playbook with others that you care about.

The first section of this Playbook will focus on the specifics of cash flow management and resources you can access on your own.

The second section of this publication focuses on my best "client getting" strategies. I believe that it is easier to grow a business if you know what works. And, that growth will be far more rewarding than any cost-cutting exercises you do.

I would rather see you grow and build a consistent business than try to reduce your costs.

Dive in! Every strategy is meant to be practical and easy to implement. Don't take my word for it, try one thing, and see if it works. Do more of what works and less of what doesn't!

Join our free LinkedIn group if you want to be part of the global Cash Flow Club movement. Don't be shy, invite your friends too!

https://www.linkedin.com/groups/14116388

CASH FLOW OVERVIEW

I will repeat this over and over. Cash flow issues are the silent killer of many businesses.

Too many simply accept the statistic that 80% of businesses fail within their first five years, and 80% of those that make it to five years fail in the next five years. That means that only 4% of businesses survive to their tenth anniversary.

That is not an acceptable success rate in any industry, why do we accept it for businesses?

The good news is that there are simple ways to improve the chances of survival for any business.

In Cash Flow Club, we focus on implementing ways to help our members:

- Increase quantity of inbound cash
- Increase speed of inbound cash
- Decrease quantity of outbound cash
- Decrease speed of outbound cash

This playbook is not meant to be exhaustive. Consider it a starting point on your journey to business wellness. Use the points here as a reference and get the help you need.

Personally, I would consider the items in this playbook as a way to start a conversation with your existing advisors in order to get the help that you need.

The most often overlooked solution to inconsistent or unpredictable cash flow is to create new revenue streams. It is cheaper and easier to introduce either new products or new services to existing clients than it is to find new clients.

Some of my favorite ways to increase the quantity of inbound cash include:

- Membership programs
- Educational content
- Increase customer average spend per purchase with new offerings
- Increase frequency of customer purchases
- Increase referrals

The best news is that many of these cash flow solutions can be implemented quickly and with immediate positive impact.

Next, we want to accelerate inbound cash flow (Inflow). The easiest ways to accelerate the speed of cash coming in is to:

- Invoice faster
- Use online tools to track and collect payments
- Offer a subscription service with clients paying monthly

Increasing the quantity and speed of inbound cash can have a dramatic effect on a business. I worked with a small electrical company that was perpetually stuck at $150,000 in annual revenues. We cleaned up their invoicing, improved cash collections, and started putting money in the bank. We were able to eliminate accounts receivables within two months. Having the cash in their bank account allowed the business to flourish. They ultimately grew to over $3 million in annual revenues.

They had been providing free financing to their clients. This "free" financing was costing them their ability to grow. Once we stopped this practice, they had the money they needed to invest in their own business.

The inflow of cash is critical to a business if it wants to survive and thrive. The outflow of cash is just as critical.

The first aspect of outflow is to decrease total outbound cash Flow. We can do this in many ways. My top three are:

- Negotiating with vendors for discounts
- Evaluating budget and Return on Investment for expenditures
- Look for preferred vendor and bulk discounts

The last area we look at in Cash Flow Club is the deceleration of outbound cash flows. We can do this by:

- Negotiating extended terms with vendors
- Matching credit type with purchase type
- Delaying non-essential payments
- Deferring non-essential purchases

I am often asked where someone should start first. That is a loaded question as it really depends on your greatest challenges in business. My first step is to get crystal clear on the inflows and outflows in your business. You must understand both their size and their timing. Once you know where your gaps are, fix the biggest problem first. Work backwards until you have a fully optimized cash generating machine.

You can watch a series of short videos on improving cash flow here:

https://youtube.com/playlist? list=PLTFNPW5g684b2GHdtjqGnC3IskqWH0b0Z

NOTES

PART 3: INBOUND CASH FLOWS

NOTES

INCREASING INBOUND CASH FLOW

For inbound cash flow or inflows, we focus on three core aspects. We want to increase the quantity of cash inflows, accelerate the speed of cash inflows, and systemize our inbound cash flow process.

We want cash flow to be predictable and reliable, which means we must be on top of the activities that lead to cash inflow.

Sadly, most businesses believe that they just have to offer a top-notch product or service and the world will throw money at them. The harsh reality is that it can be difficult to find profitable clients. And, even once you find them, you may encounter challenges in getting paid.

In this first segment, I am going to share tips on how you can improve your inbound cash flow.

NEW REVENUE STREAMS

My number one tip is to find new revenue streams. I know this might sound a little bit unusual or different. But here's the thing, it is easier and cheaper to sell more to your existing clients than it is to find new clients to sell your existing products to.

Typically, it costs six to seven times as much to acquire a new client as it does to offer more to an existing client. One of the things you need to be doing as a business is look very carefully at your products and services that you are currently offering. Find new things that you can sell or deliver to your existing clients. And by the way, sometimes the best thing you can do is create a bundle. So, for example, if you run a pet store and you typically sell caged songbirds, maybe what you could do is bundle the songbird, the food, the cage, the toys, everything into one package.

If you provide people with puppies or kittens, same thing instead of selling just the puppy or kitten, give them their first years' worth of supplies for their new pet, or include grooming with the purchase. Always be on the look out for ways to add value by removing complexity or friction.

People love new products. With the Internet, people are looking for more unique things. Find ways to deliver unique and simple.

Another thing I like to do is if you have a service-based business, create a product out of it. We create something we call a Signature System and then sell that consistently to our clients.

When you are innovating, you want to find ways to be able to reduce your inputs to reduce your costs, but the number one thing you can do to improve cash flow is to create new revenue streams.

MEMBERSHIP PROGRAMS

In my not so humble opinion, every single organization on the planet should consider how a membership program could benefit them. Don't believe me? What do you think the Public Broadcasting Service does to keep their donors engaged? What about Amazon?

The best way to create consistent inbound cash flows is to create a membership program (or programs). At the risk of repeating myself, I firmly believe that you can and should have a membership program no matter what your organization does.

The reason I like membership programs is it gives people a reason to keep coming back and it gives them a reason to pay you consistently. You can (and should) build up enough of a membership base to generate enough revenue to cover your overhead every month so that you're not always starting on the first of the month at zero.

A membership program can literally apply to any kind of business, whether you offer products or services. Everything we do nowadays comes with some element of complexity. Wouldn't it be nice if the experts shared their tips, tricks, hacks, things like that?

A few examples...

- If you are a home cleaner, your membership program might be sending your audience product samples or it might be teaching people how to remove difficult stains.
- If you are a professional service company, you can teach people how to prepare the stuff they need to bring you so that they're ready to work with you.
- If you offer products, for example, literally any product out there, you can share tips and tricks on how to improve or keep the product clean, or how to optimize use of the product.
- If you are a clothing store, you can offer your members a VIP evening for new inventory arrivals. They get to see and buy the new products first.

There are many kinds of membership programs and options. One of my absolute favorites is a "front of the line program" where you might get new products or new services, and people pay to be in front of the line so that they get to know about it first.

Think about all areas of your business and ask how you could make your life easier and make it easier for people to purchase from you. What friction or frustration can you remove? That is an area to consider as a starting point for a membership program.

One of my absolute favorite membership programs was created by John Stanton, founder of the Running Room. He created running groups to teach people not only how to run, but how to use the products that they need to be better runners. Through that he was able to scale to the point where the Running Room now has about 200 locations across North America.

People like to tell me that they can't do a membership program. Trust me you can. It's rare that I find an industry where you couldn't benefit from a membership program. We can talk about that more in a future edition of Cash Flow Club, but for now I just want to introduce the concept.

EDUCATIONAL CONTENT
The next cash flow tip we are going to talk about is creating educational content. I don't care what industry you are in; I don't care what products or services you deliver, there is always an element of education where you can add value. Ask where you can help your clients (or your

customers or your patients, whatever you call them) reduce some sort of friction or frustration in their lives.

I will share this from personal experience. I once worked with a doctor because I had a concussion. The doctor insisted on telling me all kinds of very technical things. She literally explained everything she knew about concussions to me.

You may not know this, but people with concussions are not known for their ability to remember things. Because I had a concussion, everything she told me went in one ear and out the other. The next time I would go to her office, the doctor would ask me if I had completed my homework. My response was always an honest "Sure, as far as I know, I did." I had forgotten it before I left her office on my last visit.

Rather than trusting my memory, the information would have been nice to put in a little booklet or video series or something. You should make it easy for people to follow your advice or use your product properly.

Give them something they can take away to review at home. The secret is that they will share this with other people who need your help. Make it easy for them to share you with their networks!

One of the things experts make the mistake in is assuming everybody else knows what they know about the thing they are an expert at. Think about anything that you do. I don't care if it is selling a product or delivering a service. How could you educate people to get more out of what you do?

You might be thinking, but Jeff, I install kitchen cabinets. There's no educational content. Sure, there is. You can bring in organizational experts to show people how to organize the cabinets. Have you heard about Container Store or Cabinet Genies? You can bring in cleaning experts to show people how to keep their new cabinets looking new. You can bring in designers showing people how to design a desirable living space around the cabinets.

I mean this, every product or service out there has matching educational content. Previously, I talked about John Stanton and how the Running Room created running programs. Stanton also wrote a book called "Running Start to Finish" to help his community of runners get better.

There is easily educational content for every product or service out there. And again, you're not teaching them how to necessarily do it themselves. You're teaching them how to get the most out of it. For example, if you are in the healthcare industry, you can teach people how to do the things they need to do at home to work better with you. If you are in the design industry, you can teach people how to organize their space, how to lay it out. There's educational content for everything.

And it doesn't have to be fancy, but if you can create educational content, it helps people. Educational content is a new revenue stream and it's a great way to attract new customers.

INCREASE AVERAGE SPEND

This one is probably the easiest one. Here we will talk about increasing customer average spend per purchase or visit. Believe it or not, I suspect you know this one very well.

As an example, I worked at McDonald's way back in the day when I was in high school. The number one thing we were taught was when somebody came in and ordered just a burger, we would always ask if they'd like fries with that. And then at some point, it was "would you like to make that a meal?"

What that did was very, very simple. Back in the day, a cheeseburger was about one dollar. If you added another dollar for fries, and another dollar for a drink, you tripled the average spend per purchase.

Think about your customers, and what they need. This is easy for products because if you know they buy something as a product, there's probably a cleaning product that goes along with it. For example, if they buy a new pair of shoes, you can always try to sell the shoe treatment as a bundle.

Think about what you could bundle. What could you add?

If you're offering services, let's say you're an accountant or a bookkeeper, instead of having clients spending money just to get a tax return done, maybe they will get some advice on running their business as well. Maybe have a conversation about cash flow?

What can you do? One of my favorite exercises is brainstorming around the question "How else can I add value to the customer at the point where they're purchasing?"

____

____

____

____

____

____

____

____

____

Because, as we've talked about earlier, if somebody's in front of you, they've got their wallet and their credit card out (or their debit card out), they are ready to spend. It is easier to convince them to spend a little more as opposed to spending less.

FREQUENCY

To increase the quantity of inbound cash, you want to increase the frequency of customer purchases. Some people will say, "Well, I'm a one off, or I'm a once in a lifetime purchase."

I disagree, because literally, there's no business that is a one and done. I had one person tell me that they run a funeral home and are literally the last purchase made on someone's behalf. My response is simple, the reality is, it is rarely the person who needs the funeral services that buys it. It's usually a member of the family. You can find ways, even in the funeral industry, to get repeat buying patterns established. This is a bit grim, but they sell burial plots for the family. That way, they secured the entire family as clients.

Brainstorm with your team and think about how you can increase the frequency of customer purchases. If you offer a service and they usually come to see you once a year, what could you offer them to make them come once a month? If you are a product company, you want to focus on having those consumable products. For example, you buy those coffee machines that have the little pods. You buy that machine and you are going to come back and buy the pods. Think about ways you can engineer your product or service so that people will come back to see you more often.

REFERRALS

I talk about referrals A LOT! They are literally the Gold in Your Backyard. If you are not getting referrals, you need to be clear on what you are doing wrong. Every business (or organization) should be cultivating referrals. Your best clients know your next best clients.

I have studied referrals and I am intensely fascinated by referral or word of mouth-based marketing. The challenge most people have about referrals is they think, "Oh, I get all my clients on social media, I pay for traffic." Referrals won't work for me...

The thing is, when you buying traffic, when you're paying for business leads, you still have to convert them into clients. World class sales people brag about closing 20% of those leads. That means, if you are world class at sales, you are still wasting about 80% of your marketing efforts and 80% of your sales efforts are also being wasted. You must take people from completely cold to client in as short a time period as possible.

Flipping this around, in the world of referrals, even the worst salespeople on the planet, quote statistics saying that 80 to 100% of the referrals become clients. Now, I would say you want to be probably closer to 80% (rather than at 100%). You are going to recognize that some people just aren't a fit, you can say no to those people.

The number one way to increase your referrals is to find ways to add value. We have covered a few ways to add value already. I find that the best way to increase referrals is to focus on delivering an amazing experience for every customer every time and to make it easy for them to introduce their friends and family to you. Can you give them marketing collateral or kits that they can give to friends and family to share what you do? You don't want to leave referrals to chance. Referrals are the fastest, easiest, cheapest way to grow a business. So create systems and processes to make sure you're earning referrals and following up on referrals or introductions as you get them.

INVOICE FASTER

In the previous segment, we covered some quick tips on how you can get paid more. Now, we are going to focus on how you can get paid faster.

My number one tip is invoice faster. The reason I share this tip first is a lot of businesses are relaxed around their invoicing or billing. Not you, you want to be top of mind. Your customer (or client or patient) is happiest with you at the moment you have solved the problem they came to you to solve. So, if you bill or invoice them quickly at the moment you solve their problem, they will pay you faster and they will appreciate you more. In a perfect world, get paid as soon as the service is delivered.

If you are slow to invoice, they will be slower to pay you.

As an example, I worked with an electrical company and they were taking on average one to two months to invoice their customers. The busier they were, the slower they were to invoice. By the time that invoice arrives in the mail two months later, the customer has already forgotten about how excited they were that their electrical problem was fixed. They would put it on their "I'll pay it later pile." On average, the electrical company was getting paid two to three months after they sent out their invoices. When they came to me, they were taking an average of six months to get paid.

On the flip side, they paid all their bills (including their staff) on very short terms. Typically, they paid invoices the day they received them. What we did was we started doing direct billing. The customer would have an estimate before the technician showed up at the house. When the technician showed up at the house, they had a tablet where the customer would sign off on the work done. The technician would take some pictures and add them to the customer's file. The invoice was generated immediately, and the technician would charge the customer's credit card right there. Boom, everything done, they eliminated their receivables problem almost overnight (at least stopped it from getting worse). And, yes, some people will say it costs money to accept credit cards. Usually it's two or three percent surcharge, but it's the difference between getting paid today, or six months from now.

So invoice faster is my number one tip for bringing money in the door faster. In this example, the company literally went from taking five to six months to get paid to getting paid the day they did the service. It gave them the cash flow they needed to hire more people to put in more trucks to deliver more services. They were literally able to quadruple their business in about three months time because they had cash in the bank. What could this mean to your business?

ONLINE TOOLS

We just talked about invoicing faster. Now, we are going to talk about using online tools to track and collect payments. There are great software companies out there that are doing all kinds of wonderful things. FreshBooks is one where you can invoice and get paid digitally. We also have QuickBooks Online and Xero.

These are all great tools to manage your bookkeeping and to track and collect payments. There are also payment portals out there. Instead of sending out paper invoices, you can switch to software that allows you to send out a digital proposal. When somebody accepts your proposal, their credit card is charged on the spot. Look at your industry, look at your business, and find ways to make it easier for people to pay you online.

SUBSCRIPTION

One of my favorite ways of accelerating inbound cash flow is to offer a subscription service. Your customers pay you monthly for their convenience (and yours).

I am going to break this down into two different areas. Number one, if you are a service based business, instead of getting paid once a year, productize your service to get paid monthly. How could you productize your service with a standard offering and break it down into equal monthly payments? Even if you do most of the work at one point in the year, give your clients the option to prepay throughout the year. Find service offerings that add value without costing you a lot of money. Instead of getting paid once a year by a customer, break it down into monthly payments. Having that money earlier makes a huge difference to your business. And, it also helps your clients manage their cash flow as well.

Number two, if you sell products, it is easy to break this down and improve your cash flow. A lot of people rely on customers to remember to come in and buy things. This is random and bad for your business. Better vendors remind customers to buy regularly. Personally, I think Amazon does this very well. You can have reorder points, so that certain consumable things are automatically shipped at pre-determined intervals. For example, we all use shaving cream, razor blades, shampoo, coffee, certain foods, and other things on a regular basis. Can you offer a subscription service where you send their most common purchases out on a schedule?

I know a butcher shop that once a month they do meat deliveries. Instead of relying on people to say "I haven't had beef in a while, I'm going to go to the butcher shop" they deliver it monthly. Find ways to standardize your deliveries and have that recurring revenue.

This will go a long ways to improving cash flow. We can plan more consistently if we have regular customers ordering every month. Therefore, we know we have a minimum revenue threshold.

Another example, there was a flower shop who were traditional florists. They were relying on the average person dropping in and looking for a bouquet of flowers. They found that their inventory was spoiling a lot because they're sitting there waiting for people to come in and purchase. What the florist did was find nearby offices and created a weekly bouquet delivery to be placed on the reception desk. The florist was able to double their revenue because they had these consistent revenues from their nearby customers. More importantly, they reduced their spend, especially their waste, because they knew with certainty how many flowers to order each week. They were no longer hoping somebody came in. They were delivering to known customers.

NOTES

PART 4: OUTBOUND CASH FLOWS

NOTES

DECREASING OUTBOUND CASH FLOW

For outbound cash flow or outflows, we focus on three core aspects. We want to decrease the quantity of cash outflows, decelerate the speed of cash outflows, and optimize our outbound cash flow process.

In this segment, I am going to share tips on how you can improve your outbound cash flows.

NEGOTIATING WITH VENDORS

The first tip I would share is negotiating with vendors. A lot of people are reluctant to do this, they think, "Oh, I'm going to get a bad reputation." The reality is that vendors will charge exactly as much as you allow them to, and no less. If you don't negotiate with your vendors, if you are a price taker, you are always going to pay a premium. And that's going to hurt you in the long run.

Look to your vendors and ask things like: "Do you have bulk discounts? What price would you give me if I buy and prepay? Do I get a discount? If I buy in a certain quantity, do I get a discount? If I buy older stock can I get a discount?"

We live in an age where every penny counts. We have talked about increasing cash inflows. For every dollar we bring in, we still have costs to earn that dollar. We have taxes to pay, we have expenses to pay, we have salaries to pay. For every dollar that we earn, we may end up only keeping twenty or thirty cents. But, when it comes to decreasing cash that goes out, every dollar we save is a dollar to the bottom line. I want to repeat that. The beautiful thing about saving and reducing our spending is every dollar we save goes straight to our bottom line.

We want to prioritize things like negotiating with vendors. Do you have any long term contracts that you can revisit? Do you have any vendors that would give you preferred terms if you signed a contract? If you're buying the same things repeatedly, could you set it and forget it using some sort of automatic buying and therefore get a discount? Talk to your vendors, just ask them what they can do for you.

EVALUATING BUDGET

Do you know that you must expect a Return on Investment for every dollar spent in your business?

One of the things I would strongly encourage every business out there is to create a budget. If you don't know how to create one, reach out to your bookkeeper or accountant. They can and will help you. If they won't, are you ready and willing to change your business advisors?

What the budget does is it sets the expectations and it sets the targets, and then it allows us to evaluate our decisions. If we're going to go over budget, we need to have a reason for it. If we're going to be under budget, that's great. The other thing and this ties into the budget is for every dollar spent, we need to understand what is the return on that investment.

For example, if you are spending money on an employee, typically you're looking at getting at least three or four dollars in revenue for every dollar of wage expense. If you have an employee that you're spending $50,000 a year on, and that employee is generating $50,000 of income, you have only broken even. That is not a good spend. That one employee should bring you at least $150,000 or $200,000 in revenue.

Depending on your budget, if you are doing a marketing spend, you want to look at the marketing, and as a benchmark, for every dollar in marketing you spend, that dollar should bring back ten dollars. If you spend $100 on marketing, you should earn $1,000 back in new revenues.

Look at the line items on your budget and don't get too hung up on the actual dollars. Focus on what is the Return on Investment for each line item. My best advice to you is to make decisions based on Return on Investment. The higher the return on investment, the better the decision (and spend) is for the business. The faster you get that return on investment, the better for the business, generally.

Think about both size and speed of the Return on Investment for every expense, balancing long term and short term needs of your business. And a good compromise is if something generates a reasonable return on investment in a reasonable period, that is generally a good expense for your business.

BULK DISCOUNTS

Next, we are going to talk about preferred vendor and bulk discounts. I see a lot of businesses that shop around for the cheapest deal possible, buying a bit from this vendor today, that vendor tomorrow, and another vendor next week.

Sometimes we can miss out on preferred vendor or bulk discounts. We might get a better price overall if we made all our purchases from one or two vendors. Sometimes people get very short sighted and they go around looking for the cheapest price. They are always price shopping.

Often, we can get a better deal if we say to a vendor that "over the course of the next twelve months, I am going to spend X dollars with you. What is your best price?"

Another thing a lot of people miss out on is in certain industries you might have bulk buying power through consumer purchasing groups. Reach out to any groups you are part of and find ways to get bulk discounts. This is a really, crazy one.

When I was a young lad back on the farm, we had neighbors who would come to us, and they would buy livestock for butchering. And if they couldn't necessarily afford to buy the whole animal, they would buy quarters of the animal. If you want to save money on beef, you go straight to the farm and you find four friends to split the cost with you. Each of you buys gets a quarter of an animal. It is cheaper than if you go to a butcher and buy beef by the pound.

Think about areas of your business where you could consolidate and benefit by being part of bulk buying clubs or groups.

Maybe you are in an industry where you have a bunch of collaborative, cooperative competitors. We call that coopetition. Maybe instead of each of you buying individually from one vendor, as a group, you could go together by buy a bulk order and then you split the order up and price it accordingly.

One of the things I find is if you don't ask you won't get. Go to your biggest and best vendors, the ones you buy from the most and ask them if they have loyalty programs, discount programs, prepayment programs, etc.

The thing is, if you don't ask for it, you won't get it.

NEGOTIATING WITH VENDORS (PART 2)

One of the things I find that is easiest is to find ways to slow down your cash going out. The number one thing you can do is if you are a loyal customer and you have been with the same vendor for a long time, sometimes you can ask them for terms. Generally, a vendor will offer loyal customers extra time to pay account balances. Some will allow you to pay in 30, 60, or 90 days. Some large vendors will even give you up to a year vendor financing. Obviously, you might pay a little in finance charges for that privilege.

The financing costs are usually cheaper than borrowing costs if you had to go find the money somewhere else. Reach out to your existing vendors and ask them if they will offer you preferred terms.

There is one little trick I find very useful. A lot of the credit card companies will give you 30 days to pay your balance in full and if you pay in full, you don't pay interest. One of the things you could do is negotiate with your vendors to get a 30 day term. On that final 30th day you pay your vendor balance in full by credit card. Make sure you pay it on time as you don't want to annoy your vendors. You pay by credit card and what that does is it'll give you 30 days interest free so you get 60 total days to pay something.

Negotiating with vendors is a great way to slow down your cash going out.

NEGOTIATING TERMS

The second one on our list of decelerating outbound cashflow is negotiating terms. Again, you can talk to your bank, you can get lines of credit, you can negotiate payment terms. If you don't ask you don't get.

My homework for you today is to think about all the agreements, all the places where you spend money, and reach out to your biggest vendors and ask for terms. You know, little things like with your employees, if you're paying them every week, could you pay them every two weeks? There's obviously going to be a trade off there.

If you've got a line of credit, could you pay it at the end of the month instead of the beginning of the month? If you have vendor credit, could you pay it in 30 days ? Or, will they give you a discount if you pay early?

Ask your existing vendors, the ones you have a relationship with, if they can give you better terms.

CREDIT TYPE

In this segment, we are going to talk about matching your credit type with the type of purchases you make. As an example, if you buy a building, that is a very long term asset. Presumably, you are hoping to realize the value of that asset over years or decades. In a perfect world, you want to have long term debt for a long term asset. You want to match the terms of the credit you get with the lifecycle of the property that you purchase.

Back to the building, if you are expecting to use the building for the next 50 years, you would want to have a mortgage that spans 50 years. What that does is it spreads the payments (the cash outflow) over the useful life of the asset.

Now, typically, I think most mortgages are limited to around 20 to 25 years. But that's the thing, if you buy a long term asset, like a building, even if you have the cash sitting around, it's better to borrow against the building, and then use the cash that you have sitting around either to pay off other debt. For example, you might pay off shorter term debt or higher interest debt. If you have long term debt secured by an asset, you will usually get preferred interest rates, and you are paying the debt off over a longer period. So you're not spending all of your money today and then waiting for the asset to return the investment.

I also see people buying vehicles with cash. I had one friend who, as a point of pride, paid cash for every vehicle he had owned in his life. From a cash flow point of view, you are better to have the cash in your bank invested properly, doing something productive, and borrow to finance the purchase of the vehicle. That way, you've got money on hand if you need emergency repairs, or things like that.

The biggest mistake I see people making is they use up their cash today to buy a very long term asset. The other thing I see is people will use long term debt, they'll borrow from a bank on a 10 year term, to purchase short term inventory that turns over in 30 days. So if you have inventory that turns over very quickly, typically, you'd want to purchase that on a credit card or line of credit, using short term debt for short term assets.

This is not a one size fits all, because some people are not comfortable with debt of any type. They want to know they're debt free. That's okay, as long as you always have enough money in the bank to make sure your business can go through a three to six month drought. I would challenge you if you've got assets, revisit the debt that is associated with each asset. Now if you are one of those lucky few, you've got your assets all paid off, and they're debt free. If you have a tough period, you can go to your bank and you can arrange Long Term Lending secured by long term assets or you can arrange short term lines of credit based on short term assets, like accounts receivable.

DEFERRING NON-ESSENTIAL PAYMENTS

One of the things I see when businesses are struggling is that they try to make all their payments. They try to keep everything up to date. When you are struggling, you need to triage and prioritize payments.

Things like inventory that you need to sell to stay in business, you need to prioritize those payments first. If you're paying employees to deliver services, you need to prioritize those payments next.

Anything that doesn't literally keep your lights on or keep your business moving needs to be reduced or delayed (or both).

Sometimes, especially if things are temporarily tight, you can reach out to your bank and you can ask them to defer loan payments. Some mortgages will allow you to defer your mortgage payment for a month.

Think about all your payments. This is the least exciting space because you're just slowing it down. But instead of paying everything as they come in, you might pay all your bills on the 15th and 30th of the month. So you're delaying payment by a couple of weeks. But that way it does allow you a little bit of breathing room. Similarly, if you have a vendor that offers you 60 day terms, pay on the 59th day. That's a great way to slow down the cash going out. And usually this is just enough to survive another month.

We are not going to build a business based on slowing down cash going out. This is just about keeping the lights on until we close that next deal or we get that big contract in.

DEFERRING NON-ESSENTIAL PURCHASES
The final tip in this particular series is deferring non essential purchases. This might seem obvious, but it sometimes hurts to do it. As an example, I have seen businesses that were struggling with their cash flow, and they decided that they needed to buy a new truck, or renovate the building, or update the showroom, or hire more employees.

I can't stress this enough...if you don't desperately need it today, don't buy it. Budget for it, start to save, and plan for it in the future. Look at every purchase and ask yourself whether you need to make it today to keep your lights on. If not, do not buy it, regardless of how shiny it is!

I prioritize what brings in revenue today, versus what will bring in revenue tomorrow. And I'll prioritize today revenue over tomorrow revenue, almost all the time if cash flow is tight.

NOTES

PART 5: MANAGE CASH FLOWS

NOTES

We share three core strategies for managing cash flows in Cash Flow Club. We focus on managing savings, borrowing, and investing.

We will be adding more content to this section of the book as we bring on more partners.

- Savings – what systems do you have in place to manage your savings?
- Borrowing – what systems do you have in place to manage your borrowing?
- Investing – what systems do you have in place to manage your investing?

What questions do you have for us about saving, borrowing, or investing?

____

____

____

____

____

____

____

____

____

____

____

____

____

____

____

____

____

NOTES

PART 6: CLIENT GETTING STRATEGIES

NOTES

BUILDING AUTHENTIC RELATIONSHIPS?

Building Authentic Relationships is a movement that needs to happen, it is long overdue. The past year has seen significant upheaval and rifts in society. Now, more than ever, we need to focus on Building Authentic Relationships.

Authentic Relationships are, in my opinion, essential for success in business and in life. I will share my thoughts on this and allow you to draw your own conclusions. Before we dive in, I would like to share my definitions of the words individually and collectively so that we have a common vocabulary as a starting point.

- Building - to construct by assembling and joining parts together
- Authentic - real or genuine
- Relationship - the state of being connected

To me, Building Authentic Relationships is the deliberate process of creating genuine connections between two or more people.

In every relationship and interaction, we can choose to be transactional or relationship focused. Being too transactional often means we are focused on achieving an outcome, not building a relationship with the other person. For example, buying a newspaper at a busy corner store is likely purely transactional (unless you know the person behind the counter). Being relationship focused means that you care about the other party as a human being.

I believe that we can all do more, be more, have more, accomplish more, and have more impact in life and business if we focus first on

Building Authentic Relationships. I also believe that we can be far more effective in growing our businesses by focusing on Building Authentic Relationships.

We will focus on three types of relationships that tend to have a major impact in business: clients, employees, and vendors. Let's start with clients as they are the source of our revenues. We will talk about employees and vendors in subsequent conversations.

In the past year, I have been hit with an onslaught of marketers clamoring for my attention, on behalf of businesses desperate for my attention (and money). I have been barraged on many platforms from businesses seemingly hell bent on separating me from my money, for their own personal benefit, with no regard for me as a person at all. I have removed a lot of vendors from my circle for this very reason.

I have a strange hobby, I like to engage people who are aggressive in their marketing and sales. I know it is probably a waste of time, but I do enjoy educating them about the Golden Rule.

The Golden Rule, for our purposes, is "treat others as you would like others to treat you." I always ask these aggressive marketers and sales people if they would personally respond to such tactics. For the record, I am following the Golden Rule as I would hope my friends would call me out if I was being too salesy or transactional.

I ask them to consider questions like:

- Do you personally like to be spammed?
- Would you be willing to give me your personal email address so I can put you on my list?
- Do you want to be bombarded with "buy my crap" messages at every turn?
- Would you trust a business that uses your tactics to get you as a client?

Not likely! So, why are you using these methods yourself?

If you are the one hiring a marketer or sales person, how would you personally respond to the methods that they are recommending you use? If it doesn't feel right to you, please don't condone it to get clients!

First, the bad news about clients acquired through most paid marketing channels:

- The colder the traffic the harder the sales process and ultimate sales conversation. Translation: if you get better at marketing, you need to get better at selling!
- They are less loyal, complain more, and are far more fee sensitive.
- They are significantly less likely to refer new clients to you. They assume you get all your clients through paid marketing, so they don't bother making referrals to you.
- An award winning world class sales person is ecstatic if they close 20% of the deals they get through paid marketing. Are you an award winning world class sales person?

Do you have the time, energy, and money to waste chasing leads from paid marketing? Do you have a team that can help you with this?

Now, the good news...Building Authentic Relationships is significantly cheaper and far more effective to grow a professional accounting firm (and most other businesses, for that matter).

Accountants typically tell me that they close 80 to 100% of the prospects they get through referrals. This is not by chance, Building Authentic Relationships encourages clients to refer more of their colleagues to you. Relationships that start via referrals are far more likely to result in working together than any other form of connection. Clients that come to you through relationships stay longer, are less fee sensitive and are much happier overall.

I have personally seen firms double or triple their annual revenues strictly by Building Authentic Relationships and deliberately nurturing referrals from their best clients.

Don't take my word for it, examine your own practice. Challenge me on this! Did your current best clients come through paid marketing efforts or by referral from your business network? If you are a typical firm, your best clients have come through word-of-mouth referrals.

What could you do today to start Building Authentic Relationships with your clients? Here are some examples to get you started:

- Thank you notes or cards

- Anniversary cards and/or gifts
- Customer appreciation events
- Random acts of kindness

WHAT IS CLIENTOLOGY EXACTLY?

WHY CLIENTOLOGY?

Clientology is a system for business growth that you control. You see, I have seen many businesses fail simply because they did not know how to grow and scale. More importantly, I am personally fed up with all the tactics that are simply meant to part businesses with their money, without showing any return on investment.

Clientology was created to fight back and give businesses a chance to grow AND to serve their clients better.

My goal for Clientology was that there would be no wasted time, energy, or money on the journey to success in business.

WHAT IS CLIENTOLOGY?

First things first, we must define Clientology. It is neither a cult nor a religion, it is a deliberate focus on Client Getting!

There is an art and a science to implementing the strategies of Clientology. We will share some of these in this article.

You can be forgiven for assuming that this is just another article about how to win new clients. However, it is so much more than just that.

Clientology focuses exclusively on building authority so that your Perfect Prospects chase you down. You are the prize, and you never chase.

Clientology is about balance. You want to ATTRACT Perfect Prospects, CONVERT them into Dream Clients, and DELIVER a WOW experience to earn referrals.

At the same time, you want to REPEL Nightmare Prospects, TRANSITION Nightmare Clients out, and DELIVER a WOW offloading experience to earn referrals.

The underlying theme of Clientology is earning referrals. We focus on three types of referral systems, including existing Dream Clients, Enlightened Employees, and Key Strategic Partners.

The three pillars to Clientology are: ATTRACT Perfect Prospects CONVERT them into Dream Clients and DELIVER a WOW experience to earn referrals.

When you combine all three pillars, you will have a business that grows as fast as you like, and you will have more impact, more freedom, and more joy.

Once you have the three pillars in place, you can start to build referral systems to earn referrals from Dream Clients, Enlightened Employees, and Key Strategic Partners.

The key to Client Getting is that we are consistently earning high quality referrals.

KEY STRATEGIC PARTNER PLAN

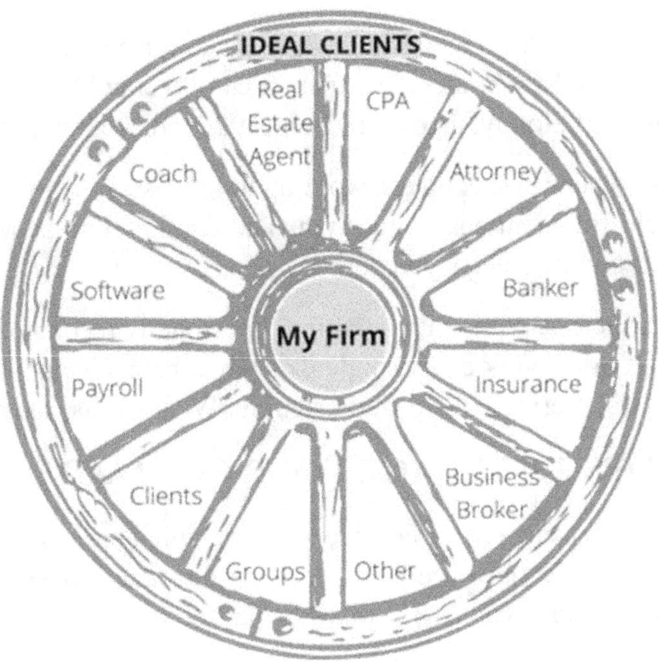

Your network is your single biggest and most valuable asset. You MUST nurture it as you would a goose that lays golden eggs. Know the difference between tactical and strategic relationships.

Tactical relationships are common in business networking today. The focus of a tactical relationship is simply on getting the very next client.

Strategic relationships will bring you a steady stream of Dream Clients over time. Treat each type of relationship with the level of respect each deserves.

When you are creating your Key Strategic Partner Plan, you must focus on building mutually beneficial quality relationships (not quantity). Your goal is to have three Key Strategic Partners per category.

There are the five steps to building your own personal Key Strategic Partner Plan. Do them in order, as one builds upon the next.

The five steps to building a Key Strategic Partner Plan are:

Step 1 - Which categories are most relevant to your business?

Step 2 - Who do you already know, like and trust that would be a great Key Strategic Partner?

Step 3 – Reach out to your network to engage with them.

Step 4 - Fill in any gaps through deliberate networking.

Step 5 – Optimize your network through ongoing contact.

The wagon wheel symbolizes your network. Your Key Strategic Partners are like the spokes, they connect you to your Dream Clients.

The three contact columns include the words Crawl, Walk, and Run for a reason. The Contact 1 column includes your favorite Key Strategic Partners. Learn to crawl here. Get really good at nurturing these relationships before you go on to Contact 2 (and eventually Contact 3).

You start by crawling with your best contacts, work up to the rest. When you are networking, don't be a referral mooch! Be intentional in receiving and giving referrals. Make sure you express gratitude to everyone who helps you out.

A great connector builds their network with intention. I personally recommend having daily habits so that you build your network every single day. Great habits include expressing gratitude, reaching out, following up, offering to help, and listening. What habits can you implement?

TIPS TO ENGAGE YOUR CONTACTS:

- Contact column 1 – these are your favorite Key Strategic Partners. You should engage with each of them at least once a month. Invite these contacts to a private LinkedIn group and regular Zoom group sessions. They will be part of your Influential Interviews and Meaningful Mastermind.
- Contact Columns 2 and 3 are invited to LinkedIn Group and weekly Zoom sessions.
- Introduce your Key Strategic Partners in each column to others in the same column. You can add enormous value to them just by doing that.

Imperfect execution is always better than perfect but incomplete. Just do it! You will get better with practice.

I love the Chinese Proverb: "The best time to plant a tree was 20 years ago. The second best time is now." In the context of Key Strategic Partners, this means that if you want success and growth in the future, the best time to act is now.

Use the image on the next page to create your own Key Strategic Partner Plan. I tell my clients all the time that it is easy to complete the Key Strategic Partner Plan. Sadly, it is just as easy to not do it.

Do you want a business that attracts a steady stream of Dream Clients? If you do, please consider creating your own personal Key Strategic Partner Plan.

I have worked with thousands of businesses. EVERY SINGLE ONE would have benefited from implementing a personalized Key Strategic Partner Plan.

Key Strategic Partner Plan

Category	Contact 1 (Crawl)	Contact 2 (Walk)	Contact 3 (Run)

RIVER OF BUSINESS

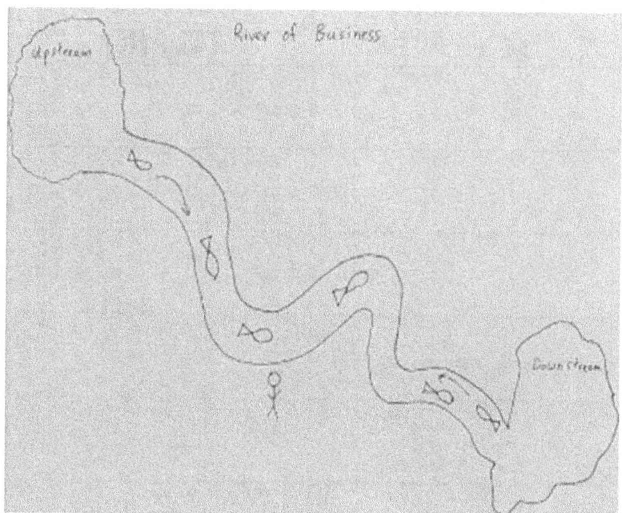

I'm going to share a little analogy that I call the "River of Business."

I run into a lot of businesspeople who are like the little stick person in the diagram (yes, I drew this myself). They stand next to the river of business waiting to catch a fish. In this analogy, the fish are clients. We will use barbless hooks and catch and release. No clients (or fish) will be harmed in the making of this analogy.

The way most people approach the river of business is to stand on the banks with their fishing gear in hand. Literally, they want a fish to stick their head out and say, "I'm hungry, please feed me." If that happens, then I will cast my line and I will hope to catch the fish.

Anybody who fishes will know that this is not a great way to catch fish. I hope, seeing this analogy, you'll understand that it is also not a great way to grow a business.

The way I view the river of business, there are two types of businesses relative to your business. There are those that are upstream and those that are downstream. The people who serve your clients after you're done with them are downstream of you. The people who serve your clients before they need your products or services are considered upstream.

For example, if I was a dog groomer, the assumption is that my Ideal Client should have a dog. Pet stores or adoption clinics would be upstream of me, the dog groomer. Downstream would probably be the people who sell the accessories, the food etc. One could argue they might be upstream of me as well. Consumables can be both upstream and downstream.

There are usually more fish coming from upstream than from downstream.

The mistake a lot of people make is they network only with people who are downstream. Then, they'll say "networking doesn't work. I did a whole bunch of networking with all of these businesses, and they never gave me a single referral." There is a scarcity mindset in there...assuming that Ideal Clients are scarce. They are abundant if you are looking in the right place.

The river of business is not one way. Just like in real life, fish will swim upstream to spawn and they will swim downstream to live out their life cycle. If we treat the River of Business as an ecosystem. We can (and should) put our efforts into building relationships with those both upstream and downstream of our business. Upstream businesses may inform you that they just sent a school of fish your way and you should get your nets in the water. And, we can do the same for our downstream partners.

We are custodians of the ecosystem. Part of our job is to maintain our ecosystem. And that's how you get referrals. First, you build the ecosystem with those upstream, but you also build an ecosystem with those downstream. You might be thinking that this sounds like work. It isn't, you only need to reach the magic number of 11 other businesses in this ecosystem with you (roughly half upstream and half downstream).

The key to this is understanding who your Ideal Client is, what they need, how they move from the beginning to the end. We want to play nice in our ecosystem. We are custodians, we need to protect our ecosystem. We're going to prevent pollution. We're going to prevent overfishing. We're going to make sure that there's breeding stock that can keep spawning. We are in fact, watching over this ecosystem. We don't own it. We are there as a steward or as a guide.

When you're building your Key Strategic Partner network, you want to think about 12 people (including yourself). A total of 12 is the magic number. The reason it's 12 is if we did a monthly series, everybody could speak for one of the months in the year.

The reality is I don't know a lot of businesses that can handle more than a dozen referral partners. Your role as a steward of the ecosystem is to pick your 11 favorite people. I will share here that curating a list of great businesses in your ecosystem adds value to you, your referral partners, and to your clients. If you understand who's upstream of you and who's downstream, it adds value to you and to the entire ecosystem. Most importantly, it adds value to the fish. Instead of just randomly dropping the fish back in the river and saying good luck, you can say to that fish, "you need to go stop at this point, this point, this point." You can add value to your ecosystem by guiding the fish safely on their journey.

RELATIONSHIP MARKETING

In my opinion, relationship marketing is one of the best kept secrets in the marketing world.

Traditional marketing efforts focus almost exclusively on the acquisition of new customers. The challenge is that it is more expensive to acquire a new customer than it is to maintain an existing customer and get them to spend more with you.

Traditional marketing has another major challenge. It is widely held in the marketing and sales world that a world class sale professional, one who wins awards, closes at most 20% of their deals from paid traffic.

Most local businesses are not run by world class sales professionals. Sadly, you can expect your closing rate to be substantially lower unless you fall into the discounting to earn the business trap. In that case, your business (and life) might actually be worse off if you end up landing a really price sensitive client.

The secret to success in business is to attract better clients, not just "more. The marketing giants do not want to you focus on better, they make money selling you more.

Better clients means that you can grow your business, work less, have more impact, and generally enjoy your life more.

More clients simply means that you might just end up doubling your business. Doubling generally means that you double your headaches too.

There are many reasons why you might want to focus on relationship marketing to attract better clients. I will share my personal top five here.

- Relationship marketing is generally either free or low cost to implement.
- Relationship marketing provides perpetual results when you do it right. That means you will have a reliable, predictable, steady stream of Dream Clients coming to your business when you need them.
- Relationship marketing increases the length of relationship you have with existing (and new) clients and they spend more with you over the lifetime of your relationship.
- A client who comes to you through relationship marketing is more likely to be more loyal and more understanding. They will forgive mistakes faster.
- Existing clients who refer new clients to you are statistically more likely to be more loyal, more forgiving, and far less fee sensitive. They will spend more with you over a longer period of time.

The biggest challenge that I see with relationship marketing is knowing where to start. The good news is that once you start, you will see results as long as you stay vigilante and nurture your most important relationships with your existing best clients.

I would challenge each of you to ask yourselves, what would have to change if my business were to be by referral only? When it comes to referrals, you must follow all three of these steps:

1. Earn - you must give your clients a reason to speak about you over and above the services that you offer. White glove service helps this along the way.
2. Ask - make sure you are finding the right ways to ask for referrals.
3. Thank - gratitude is everything with referrals. You must focus on the relationship and encourage your clients to do the same. The fastest way to make sure referrals dry up is to forget to say thank you.

We have a "Stay in Touch" Program that we use. We send out a seasonal card to our best clients every month. We use the cards to remind our clients that they matter.

Here is just a sample of what we might do in a given year. The key is that we have a system in place and we follow it.

- January - send a "new year" greeting card
- February - Valentine theme - we love our clients
- March - celebrate Spring
- April - celebrate Jazz Appreciation Month
- May - celebrate Mothers
- June - celebrate Fathers
- July - celebrate Independence Day
- August - celebrate warm summer days
- September - celebrate Autumn
- October - celebrate Halloween
- November - celebrate the holidays
- December - invite to a client celebration

The goal of our Stay in Touch program is to show our clients that we are thinking of them. They will then think of us when someone is looking for our services. We also include a monthly newsletter in our program. This allows us to share valuable content that our clients can share with their friends and family.

We make it easy to refer to us by staying top of mind. If you are like me, you are thinking that this sounds like a lot of work. Buying cards, envelopes, and stamps feels like enough to end the program before it even begins. Forget about the extra effort of actually filling out and addressing the cards.

Allow me to introduce you to a program called Send Out Cards. They have created a simple process to easily fill in and send cards. You create and personalize your cards online and they take care of the rest. They handle the printing and mailing of the cards at a very reasonable price. Here is my affiliate link if you want to explore Send Out Cards on your own: https://www.SendOutCards.com/u/jborschowa.

Or, you can just visit https://www.SendOutCards.com if you don't like affiliate programs.

DIGITAL MAGAZINES

In the last article, we discussed the importance of Relationship Marketing.

Our Stay in Touch program has two key elements, physical greeting cards and digital magazines.

Before we get into the details, I want to share the mindset that goes into our Stay in Touch Program. Studies have shown that it is cheaper to grow a business by converting existing clients into raving fans. Raving fans bring their friends to a business. We will also discuss what not to do.

Raving fans and their friends are the best way to grow and scale any type of business. They spend more, value you more, and appreciate what you do for them...all while bringing more like them. You can literally clone your best clients.

There is a common assumption that all clients are created equal. Test this statement, it is RARELY true. I have done this over and over with my clients and have proven it 100% of the time (so far).

If we apply the Pareto Principle, it is safe to say that 20% (or less) of your customers bring in the majority of your revenues. On the flip side, it is equally likely that the bottom 20% of your customers cause the most problems and complain the most.

The goal behind the Stay in Touch program is to make it easy for our best clients to share who we are, why we exist, and what we do with their friends, family, and colleagues.

The Digital Magazine concept that we use is focused on adding value to anyone who reads them, regardless of whether they end up doing business with us or not.

Sadly, most people focus on the wrong metrics for a digital magazine. They mistakenly believe that it is like any other magazine out there, focusing solely on distribution or other vanity numbers.

To be very blunt, we do not care about distribution or vanity numbers. Our primary driver is to add value.

We add value to our contributors, our advertisers, our partners, and most of all to our readers. You see, if we focus on making everyone's world better for having met us, we will never want for business. As you read through our magazine, see if you can find examples of how we add value.

KEYS TO SUCCESS WITH A DIGITAL MAGAZINE:

- Focus on value - how can you improve someone's world for them graciously sharing their time with you? There are three easy ways to add value to another person. First, you can share a resource that solves their problems directly. Second, you can guide them to other resources that might solve their problem for them. Thirdly, you can connect them with a network that might contain someone who can help them.

- Give without depleting - most professionals, coaches, consultants, and advisors give away too much in one to one meetings. They share ideas and years of experience freely and willingly. This is a great mindset, but it often leaves the "giver" feeling depleted. A digital magazine allows you to answer questions without taking up your previous time. And, once created, is something of value that can be shared over and over.
- Fall in love with your clients, not your solution - it is completely acceptable to promote your products and services in your digital magazine. However, if you are only promoting, you aren't adding value. Sometimes you will encounter a problem that you cannot solve for your clients. Find another expert who has a solution that you can trust and share it. The more you love your clients, the easier it is to solve their problems. The more problems you solve, the more they will happily pay you and refer you to others.

Focus on connections, not "distribution" - the most important relationships you can nurture with a digital magazine are your Key Strategic Partners (have them contribute articles), your advertisers (help them win), your clients (share content they need), and the world at large. You have no idea where your next best client might come from. Why not put value out in the world so that they can easily find you? If you become a trusted resource, they will come to you should they ever need help.

KEYS TO FAILURE WITH A DIGITAL MAGAZINE (WHAT NOT TO DO):

- Oversell - if you cross the line and sell too much, you will end up not selling anything. Nobody wants to be sold, but everybody loves to buy. Remember that as you are creating content. Share great ideas and the occasional offer. A good rule of thumb is that at least three quarters of your content should be truly quality information and at most one quarter should be promotional. We strongly encourage you to make sure even your promotional materials are quality information.
- Focus on the self - a Digital Magazine that is ego- centric and all about you will fail. Try to find the right balance. For example, we have many articles in this edition that seek to serve even if we never end up doing business together. Every editorial and graphic design decision we make is focused on our readers and how we might be able to add more value to them.
- Vanity metrics - many large publications focus on distribution and readership numbers. They do this so that they can charge more for their advertisements. Adding value to your specific readers, even if it is only the small group of content creators, is the best way to measure success. If I can help one person solve a problem, that is a win for me.

BUSINESS LUNCHES

"Would you like to meet for lunch?"

This is not a new question, it has been around since the dawn of business. Is it still relevant today?

The world shut down during the COVID-19 Pandemic. The simple things, like having lunch with friends, became challenges.

A lot of businesses suffered during COVID. My goal is to help where I can.

Most of my business growth efforts are accomplished over lunch. You might wonder why, so allow me to share my thoughts.

Historically, we "broke bread" with friends and allies. We rarely sat across a table and dined with our sworn enemies. To dine with someone is the fastest way I know of to get to know them and for them to get to know me.

It might seem cliché , but people still buy people before they buy products or services.

Building authentic relationships will build a long-term business with predictable and sustainable growth.

I know with certainty that meeting the right great people and building authentic relationships with them will help me in all aspects of life. For now, let's just focus on business.

We are social creatures. We all crave belonging and acceptance at some level. Hosting lunch is a great way to foster the relationships and build in acceptance and belonging.

The secret to a great business lunch is to follow a few simple guidelines. I will go into that more on the next page.

A lot of people dismiss the power of lunches because of misguided beliefs. The single biggest myth is that business lunches do not work. The next myth is that they do not produce reliable, predictable, or scalable results. We will address both myths.

GUIDELINES FOR SUCCESS WITH LUNCH:
- Agenda - have a stated agenda up front. I particularly like to set the stage for what will happen. I share this "agenda" in the invitation. Typically, it is worth noting that the goal is to get to know one another to share connections (if that is your goal). If the goal is to sell something to someone, make sure you are clear on that up front too. Trust me, there is nothing worse to a networking professional than to walk into an unexpected sales pitch. Remember, build relationships first, the deals will naturally follow.
- Participants - be strategic in who you invite. Assuming you have built your Key Strategic Partner Plan, make a point of always inviting one to join you for lunch when you are meeting new people. And, always ask your new person to bring a friend.   That way, you all leave with new connections.

- Consistency - when I am actively growing a business, I focus on consistency. I know that meeting people for lunch will build the relationships that I need in order to succeed. And, I know that I can add value to my connections by connecting them to one another. I schedule a weekly lunch date (same time, same location, new people). That way, I don't have to pull out my calendar. I can tell people to join me at a given place on a given date. This little trick will save you hours of time!
- Giving - do not expect to receive before you give. Connect people with no expectation other than to be of service. The universe will reward you for this. Make deliberate introductions to people who can help one another.
- Mindset - I personally believe in the mindset of "Giver's Gain" and "The Go-Giver." Decide who and how you best wish to serve through your business lunches.

MYTHBUSTING

- Business lunches do not work...I hear this one all the time. And, there is some merit to this myth. I see a lot of people who approach business lunches with no forethought or intention. You cannot hope to hit a target if you have no idea what the target is. Before you undertake a business lunch strategy, you need to be really clear on your objectives. This should include who you will meet, how often you will meet, for how long you will meet, and what you expect as an outcome of the meeting. A little bit of clarity will carry you a long way.
- Business lunches do not produce reliable, predictable, or scalable results. This one is a particular favorite of mine. The assumption underlying this is that there is a better alternative. The reality is that business lunches done well are un-matched in their ability to produce reliable, predictable, and scalable results. The secret is to have an agenda, choose your participants carefully, consistently schedule lunches, show up with a giving attitude, and have a mindset of service. Does any of that sound familiar? You are correct, the main source (and fuel) for this myth is simple ignorance. Not knowing how to do something well makes it too easy to dismiss the thing.

I will share a parting story. I have a friend who was on the sales team of a billion dollar company. He and his hundreds of colleagues were tasked with finding new clients for the company's latest product launch. Many of the sales people did what they knew best...they grabbed the phone and started cold-calling. Some had quick wins, but few had lasting success. My friend started a networking group. Within a month, he was top of the leaderboards and stayed there. He invited his best clients to join him for lunch once a week and bring their friends. His Perfect Prospects pursued him.

AUTHORITY BOOKS

Clientology is based on the fundamental principle of establishing our authority to attract Perfect Prospects and serve our Dream Clients to the very best of our abilities.

To be an authority simple means that we demonstrate our ability to help people in our specific area of expertise. We truly believe that the fastest way to be seen as an authority in your field is to AUTHOR a book. You literally cannot spell AUTHORity without the word author.

In terms of writing an AUTHORity Book, you could do it yourself. You could do what I did. I spent hours and hours and hours and honestly, weeks and months, studying the concept of writing a book and thinking about what I needed to include. I also had to think about what I should exclude from the book. You can do all of this yourself.

But the reality is, do you have the time to do all that research, and then hopefully produce a book that gets results?

The biggest risk with writing an AUTHORity Book by yourself is that you can put in a lot of effort and not get results from it. Or, worse, you could spend months writing and never finish the book.

If you write your own AUTHORity book, you will have to go through the trial-and-error process and test things to see what will either succeed or fail.

The next risk is the actual length of timeline. I know for a fact that it takes a lot longer to write your first book than to write your second, third, and so on. My first book took me two years to write. I can now write one in under a month.

Time in terms of hours is another risk of writing an AUTHORity book by yourself. How long is it going to take you to distill your knowledge into a book that gets you clients? That is the thing I want to stress when we talk about books. We are talking about an authority piece that gets you clients.

We are not talking about sharing everything you know about a topic. I made that mistake with the first book that I wrote. I wrote it as a professional guide to help other accountants and bookkeepers implement technology in their business. I spent a lot of time, and the first book took me two years to get out to the world. I taught everything I knew about the subject. That is good if you are writing university textbooks. The sole goal of an AUTHORity Book is to get you clients. You want your AUTHORity Book to answer the questions that your prospects have, not that your colleagues have.

What I mean by that is, when I wrote my first book, helping accountants and bookkeepers, I tried to answer all their questions. This led me down this rabbit hole of helping other accountants and bookkeepers. I had originally intended for the book I was writing to help small businesses in general. I got lost on who my audience was, and I was so focused on accountants and bookkeepers that I lost sight that I was passionate about helping small business.

My goal is very simple. Every AUTHORity Book that I produce should get me clients. That is literally its sole purpose. There are many ways to accomplish this sole purpose, but we must always keep the end goal in mind.

When we write an AUTHORity Book for a potential client, we want to help them answer three important questions:

1. Do I have the problem that the author solves?
2. Do I want to solve the problem?
3. Is the author the right expert to help me solve my problem?

Your AUTHORity Books will be intentionally short and will answer these three questions for your Perfect Prospect.

I know that you might be thinking that this is very self- serving for the author. You are partially correct. The author is helping themselves by taking the time to be clear about who they serve, what problems they solve, and how they solve them. The author's business will improve just through the act of writing their AUTHORity Book. And, yes, the author will receive Dream Clients from their AUTHORity Book. However, every AUTHORity Book begins with one assumption - the person reading the book must receive value greater than the hour (or so) of their life that they are giving up. We offer tips to improve their lives and guidance on avoiding common pitfalls.

Remember, all aspects of Clientology focus on building authentic relationships in business. We focus on adding value to our Perfect Prospects and help them decide if they want to become our next Dream Client. Whether they choose to work with us or not, we leave them better for having known us.

I will let you in on a little secret. If your intention for writing a book is to improve your own personal status, that will be the outcome. You will benefit, but others might not. If you start with an intention to serve, your book will serve others and you in the process.

A friend of mine shared a saying that I love: "You can't out-give the universe." A book is a great gift to give the world and it will come back to you many times over if you do it right!

INFLUENTIAL INTERVIEWS

Influential Interviews are commonly referred to as podcasts. However, as with all things in Clientology, we have a fundamental twist that sets us apart.

You see, most podcasts are solely about the person who has the podcast. They benefit from interviewing guests and sharing it with their audience. Traditional podcasters tend to focus on vanity metrics like audience size, downloads, reviews, etc.

Influential Interviews are different from the outset. Our primary focus, as always, is on building authentic relationships with Key Strategic Partners, our audience, and the world at large.

Our Influential Interviews are conversation starters with our Key Strategic Partners and help us solve problems for our Perfect Prospects and Dream Clients.

When we win, everybody wins. We introduce our Key Strategic Partners to our network, we get to know our Key Strategic Partners, and in turn we can introduce our Key Strategic Partners to one another.

Influential Interviews help us build our authority while we help our Key Strategic Partners build theirs.

The biggest challenge with Influential Interviews is knowing how to do it correctly. You can literally waste a lot of time, , and money if you are not careful and deliberate.

As in all business activities, the most important step is to get really clear on who you serve and what problems you solve for them. This will guide all that you do with your Influential Interviews.

You can read this article and my book on Influential Interviews if you want to figure things out by yourself.

For what it is worth, I have spent hours and hours, weeks, and months of my life, three or four years, learning everything I can about creating a podcast.

Influential Interviews truly are a fancier podcast format. The problem is that I see a lot of broke podcasters out there.

The goal of our podcast is not to be famous for the sake of famous, it is not there to help us spread our ego.

The goal of the Influential Interviews is again to get us clients and build our authority.

Back to trial and error, I went through all the iterations, I tested out things. I wasted a lot of time, a lot of energy, a lot of money trying to figure out the podcast.

The secret is, and I give you this as a secret so that you can do it yourself. The guests you have on the podcast are as important as the audience you serve. If you are a professional service firm, or you are selling products, or whatever you are doing, you want to be really, really clear who your Dream Client is. You want to offer value to them through the guests on your podcast.

As an example, if you are an accountant who wants to work with plumbers in Atlanta, you would interview other people that offer value to those plumbers. You might bring on somebody who can help them with reputation management, help them increase their online reviews, which would be something of value to the audience.

I believe that all value should be multifaceted. In this case, we are going to add value to the audience by bringing in other experts.

We add value to the other experts by sharing their message with our audience.

We can add a lot of value to our experts by introducing them to one another. Being the hub of a local expert network will give you a permanent advantage in your specific market.

And then lastly, we benefit because we are seen hanging out in our space with other experts in our space. And we are also learning more about our audience and what they do and what they think and the problems they have.

I would argue, especially if you are professional, you should fall in love with one industry niche and really focus on all their problems, even the ones you do not solve. Because by being the expert and looking at it from the 30,000-foot level, you can bring them speakers and content that adds value to them.

The real value is that your community benefits because you are bringing information into the light, helping people not just learn things, but also to implement things.

If you are doing a podcast, that is the number one secret is knowing what your audience is, knowing who your strategic partners are, and really focusing on how you can add value. The other secret is why would somebody recommend your podcast to others?

Think about the podcast as your outreach. If somebody wants to know more about you, then they are going to Google you, they are going to search out, they will watch a podcast to see if you are somebody they want to get to know. And again, if they see you spending time together with other experts, they are going to want to know you.

MEANINGFUL MASTERMINDS

Masterminds are the greatest force for good on the planet. We can learn new things, meet new people, and solve problems together. Two minds are better than one!

Meaningful Masterminds are the third element of Clientology. Like the other elements of Clientology, the focus of Meaningful Masterminds is to build authentic relationships with your Key Strategic Partners, team members, clients, and community at large.

The biggest risk of creating Meaningful Masterminds yourself is time.

I have personally spent years becoming an expert in masterminds. I would argue that my journey is just beginning, it is not ever going to be over as far as I am concerned.

The key to the mastermind is having the right types for the right people.

I believe that every business could benefit from having three types of masterminds. One to attract people into your universe, one to convert people from prospect into dream client. And then the third one is to figure out how to deliver Wow.

In Clientology™, we have a three-part mastermind concept called ATTRACT, CONVERT, and DELIVER.

You want to add value to all parties at all stages. The difference is a lot of people will have what they call a "mastermind group" but it is anything but a mastermind group.

The biggest mistake you can make is to have a poorly executed mastermind group. This will cause you more harm you in the long run rather than help you. A good mastermind has a very clear goal upfront, focused on answering the question "what are we hoping to accomplish from the mastermind?" Secondly, it has a very curated guest list.

This is not a random open house; you do not want a large group of people joining it. Your mastermind needs to be selective and exclusive. When you are doing the mastermind, for example, on delivering the wow, you want your best customers in the room, because you want feedback on how to make it better for them.

The biggest risk with a mastermind, if you do it yourself, is, you can waste a lot of time on it, for example learning how to run a mastermind.

I have taught hundreds of people how to run masterminds. In my experience, very few go on to do them well. And really, it is because you cannot learn mastermind facilitation in a book. You need to learn it doing it.

It is one of those cases where you must be brave enough to just jump out of the airplane and then pull the cord on your parachute. You need to learn in the process. You cannot think about it, you cannot overanalyze it, you must just do it. And that is the biggest thing you can waste a lot of time thinking about launching a mastermind or debating about launching. We help our clients launch their first mastermind quickly and perfect it as they go.

My goal for Meaningful Masterminds is very simple. We want to build authentic relationships with our Key Strategic Partners AND find new ways to add value to our community of Perfect Prospects and Dream Clients. Simple to do, simple to not do, and a massive competitive advantage for everyone who participates.

Building authentic relationships with Key Strategic Partners, Perfect Prospects, and Dream Clients is literally the sole purpose of Meaningful Masterminds. There are many ways to accomplish this sole purpose, but we must always keep the end goal in mind.

When we host Meaningful Masterminds with our Key Strategic Partners, we are helping one another find ways to build value for our Perfect Prospects and Dream Clients. The more value we as a collective create, the more Perfect Prospects we will attract. And the longer our Dream Clients will stay with us.

Overall, our intent is to make everyone in our Key Strategic Partner community highly referrable.

Your Meaningful Mastermind meetings will be intentionally short and will focus on finding new ways to add value.

We generally ask three questions over and over:

1. How can we add value to our community of Perfect Prospects?
2. How can we serve our Dream Clients to our fullest?
3. What other challenges do our Perfect Prospects and Dream Clients face that we can solve through our network and connections?

As in all aspects of Clientology, we all win together. Building authentic relationships happens quickly and first. Doing business is the secondary by-product. The intention to serve makes all the difference in how well you will succeed.

I cannot stress this enough, if you are looking to receive first, Clientology and its tools will not work for you.

NOTES

PART 7: OUR SIGNATURE SYSTEM

NOTES

OVERVIEW OF OUR SIGNATURE SYSTEM

Our clients have high standards and so do we. We believe that a great Signature System is the only way to deliver world class results reliably and predictably for our clients. Our Cash Flow Management Process has been designed to ensure that every single client gets the same high level of service that they deserve, while we deliver the results that they expect.

Our Cash Flow Management Process has five stages:

- Stage 1: Diagnose
- Stage 2: Recommend
- Stage 3: Implement
- Stage 4: Maintain
- Stage 5: Optimize

We will go into more detail for each stage.

STAGE 1: DIAGNOSE

Unfortunately, many of our competitors skip this stage entirely and they go straight into the tactics they are most comfortable with. They end up treating your business just like everyone else's business.

I know you are probably thinking right now "yes, but my business is different." We agree with you 100%.

We conduct a Strategy Session with every client so that we know exactly what your goals are, how your business operates, and how we can assist you. We take the time at the beginning to get to know you and your business so that we can tailor our recommendations for your business.

We will create a Strategic Vision Plan specifically for you. Your Strategic Vision Plan will give you a quick overview of where you are, where you want to be, and the shortest path between the two.

Tactics Versus Strategies

Tactics are usually tasks or small projects that help you achieve a short-term goal. For example, filing a tax return is a common short-term goal for most small businesses.

Strategies are usually long-term projects that help you achieve long term objectives.

The mistake most businesses make is to focus on individual tactics, without any real consideration for the overall long-term objectives of the organization.

Our Strategic Vision Plan helps you understand the difference. Tactics implemented without strategy may have you fighting the wrong battles. Strategy without tactics will leave you stagnant and wondering what went wrong. The best tactics are inspired by the strategies needed to achieve long term goals.

STAGE 2: RECOMMEND

Once we summarize your Strategic Vision, our team starts to build out your Bulletproof Business Blueprint. The recommendations that we make will be based on the shortest path to accomplishing your long-term goals. We pride ourselves on strategic thinking and immediate execution to achieve results.

We will recommend the right combination of long-term strategy and short-term tactics to help you accomplish your business growth goals.

We specialize in local businesses who want to maximize their growth. Our team of experts will recommend a tailored approach for your specific business.

To be successful in business, you need to have a business growth plan that you have created with intention and that you nurture and grow. We will help you create that quickly.

STAGE 3: IMPLEMENT

Once we agree on the path forward, our team leaps into action to help you implement. We offer a range of implementation programs. Our top three are:

Do It Yourself

Perhaps you know what you need to do or have a team member who can do the work, but you need a bit of help creating a strategy. We can give you the strategy and leave the implementation in your hands. We only do this if we truly believe this is the best option for your business.

Full disclosure, the "do it yourself" model is our cheapest model for a reason. In our experience, very few businesses have the necessary skills to implement on their own.

Done With You

This is our most popular option. With this option, we provide you with the Strategic Plan and guide you through implementation. Consider our team your project manager as you implement on your own. We are available to guide you and answer any questions that you may have.

Done For You

Our absolute best offering is the "done for you" model. Here, we take care of every detail so that you can focus on running your business. You do what you do best, and we will help you grow.

Done for you is not for everyone. We do the work to ensure that you get the best possible results in the shortest time possible. This level of expertise comes at a premium cost. However, we believe that every business expenditure should have a predictable return on investment. The goal is to maximize this return, not minimize the cost for a successful business plan.

Regardless of the level you choose, we are here to support your business in achieving your goals.

STAGE 4: MAINTAIN

Business should be boring and predictable. If you want excitement in your life, take up a hobby like skydiving or fire breathing. Inconsistency and unpredictable results are major sources of stress in any business.

With our "set it and forget it" maintenance program, you know with certainty that you will get consistent and predictable results every month.

Our team will work with you to ensure that your goals are being met and that your long-term objectives are being realized.

STAGE 5: OPTIMIZE

Our final stage is possibly our most unique stage. We find that a lot of our competitors will help you with implementation and maintenance, but they don't have a system in place for optimization.

In our Optimize phase, we meet with you on a regular basis to ensure that we are not only solving the challenges you hired us to solve, but we are helping you identify additional challenges BEFORE they become a big problem.

We have a quarterly review process where we ensure that you are still on track to meet your long-term objectives. More importantly, we review your long-term objectives to make sure they still fit. And we review your business to look for any untapped potential or areas for growth.

Consider us a partner in your business. We leverage our Optimize stage to ensure that we are finding new ways to add value to your business every quarter.

Do your current advisors share their process with you?

____

____

____

____

____

____

____

____

How would it feel working with someone who shares their process with you up front?

____

____

____

____

____

____

OUR CORE STRATEGIES

We leverage three core strategies to help you build a community of raving fans. We will go into greater detail on each of these in the remainder of this book.

• Influential Interviews

• AUTHORity Books

• Signature Systems to deliver WOW experiences

We leverage these three strategies because they consistently deliver great results for our clients, literally in every industry. We believe that building a community of raving fans is the best way to grow with intention and to create long lasting results.

GET HELP WITH YOUR STRATEGIC VISION PLAN

I have shared throughout this book how you can benefit from implementing a Strategic Vision Plan by yourself. I have done this as having a basic plan in place is far better than having no plan at all. If you want help, my experienced team and I can assist you in taking the necessary action to create a customized Strategic Vision Plan for your business. Reach out to our team and use the content of this book to start the conversation.

Scan the QR Code or go directly to our website here:

https://www.globalwellnesshq.com/cash-flow-club

NOTES

PART 8: CASH FLOW CLUB LOGISTICS

HOW CASH FLOW CLUB IS STRUCTURED

Cash Flow Club is structured as a combination of mastermind program, recorded trainings, and online community. We have structured Cash Flow Club to ensure that you receive all the help you require when you need it.

WHAT IS A MASTERMIND PROGRAM?

"You are the average of the five people you spend the most time with." ~ Jim Rohn

"…a friendly alliance with one or more persons who will encourage one to follow through with both plan and purpose." ~ Napoleon Hill

WHAT A MASTERMIND PROGRAM IS

- Formal, structured, and focused
- Consistent – scheduled on a regular basis
- Productive, encouraging, and inspiring
- Brutally honest – tell you what you need to hear
- A place of trust

WHAT A MASTERMIND PROGRAM IS NOT

- A cult
- A business partnership
- A gossip group
- A party
- A whine fest

BENEFITS OF A MASTERMIND PROGRAM

- Results
- Accountability
- Encouragement
- Inspiration
- Outside feedback
- Unbiased opinions
- You will grow together

WHAT ARE MASTERMINDS LIKE?

- Maximum 24 people
- Share same values and goals
- People who are willing to dissect and be dissected
- No "know-it-alls"
- Participants should be plus or minus two levels of each other
- If a participant is too advanced, they may feel like they are always providing information, getting nothing out of it (free consultation)
- If a participant is too low, they may be seen as a taker, nothing to contribute

MASTERMIND ROLES
- The Moderator
- The Hot Seat
- The Group

THE MODERATOR
- One person from previous meeting's hot seat
- Keep track of time
- Direct the conversation
- Prompt the quiet ones

THE HOT SEAT
- Assigned in advance
- Present a problem or issue
- Talk about current or upcoming projects
- Present a recent finding or discovery
- Ask specific questions for group

THE GROUP
- Listen and pay attention
- Share experiences and resources
- Dissect and investigate further
- Ask probing questions
- Encourage and support

BUILDING WINNING MASTERMIND GROUPS
1. Be brutally honest (and respectful)
2. Share how YOU are best motivated
3. Dedicated GOALS meetings (twice per year)
4. Plan ahead when you are in the hot seat
5. If online-based, meet in person at least once per year
6. Start a private hub for sharing
7. Follow up and know it is okay to disagree
8. Make it a priority (put it in your calendar)
9. Make rules for the group
10. What happens in the Mastermind stays in the Mastermind (sacred place)

CASH FLOW CLUB MASTERMIND GROUND RULES

- Unimportant decisions made by consensus.
- Important decisions are made by group vote.
- Our group is not group therapy or whining.
- Complaining or gossiping will not be tolerated.
- You can miss up to one meeting per quarter. Every effort should be made to attend.
- Members may come and go as their needs change. We will introduce new members if the group drops below 12 active participants.
- Confidentiality is critical to the success of this group. Everything here is sacred and must not be shared outside of the group.
- Group majority will determine if we need to have a non-disclosure agreement.
- We ask for a commitment to honesty, integrity, trust, and respect for all members.
- We ask members to be self-aware and to not try to dominate the conversation or give orders.
- Leave your ego at the door.

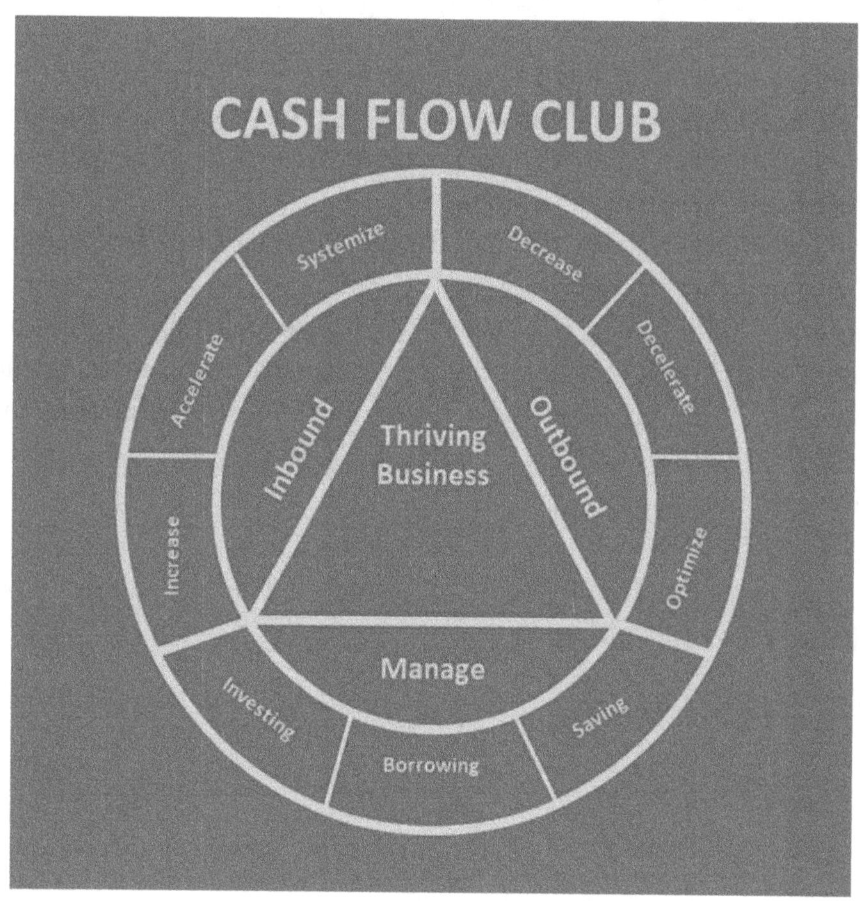

The key to a thriving business is to be in complete control of your cash flows. We teach our Cash Flow Club members how to manage all aspects of their cash flow by leveraging our Inbound, Outbound, Manage framework.

JOINING CASH FLOW CLUB

1. Read this book or attend our workshop.
2. Complete our Clarity Worksheet.
3. Complete our Strategy Worksheet.
4. You decide – is Cash Flow Club a fit for you?
5. We decide – are you a fit for Cash Flow Club?
6. Schedule a Strategy Session.

CASH FLOW CLUB WORKSHOP

We will share strategies and practical tips that business owners and entrepreneurs can implement immediately to improve the overall cash flow in their business.

We will talk about inbound cash flow, outbound cash flow, and managing cash flows overall.

In 90 minutes, we will share:

- How to increase the volume of inbound cash flows, accelerate the speed of inbound cash flows, and systemize inbound cash flows for greater business certainty.
- How to decrease the volume of outbound cash flows, decelerate the speed of outbound cash flows, and optimize outbound cash flows for great business strength.
- How to manage saving, borrowing, and investing in a business.

WELCOME TO THE CASH FLOW CLUB!

We created the Cash Flow Club to help local business owners grow and scale their business.

Most businesses that fail do so because of cash flow issues. Our goal is to give you immediate and practical advice that you can implement in your business today.

Some of the ideas will have a huge impact, some will have a small impact. BUT, if you implement enough, your business will thrive.

We will focus on three core areas of cash flow:

- Inbound Cash
- Outbound Cash
- Managing Cash for the long-term.

We have designed Cash Flow Club as a monthly subscription. You can join us for as long as you like and you can leave at any time.

We guarantee that you will more than get your money's worth if you implement just one of our ideas each month.

CASH FLOW CLUB MEMBERSHIP OPTIONS

Pick the membership option that best fits your needs:

1. Month to Month Basic Membership: This allows you to test the waters and see if you want to join us full on. The month to month option includes membership access to our private online community and the weekly calls.
2. Full Year Prepaid Basic Membership: There is no discount to prepay. However, if you commit fully to us, we commit fully to you. We will send you a special welcome package (plus a few more surprises). You will also receive access to our private online community and the weekly calls.
3. Month to Month Silver Membership: Our silver membership includes unlimited access to our weekly recorded trainings. We share at least one valuable lesson per week via recorded content. The focus will be on immediately actionable tips that you can leverage today to grow your business.
4. Month to Month Gold Membership: Our gold membership includes everything in our basic and silver memberships. We include weekly live Q&A calls that are exclusively for our Gold Members.
5. Month to Month Elite Membership: This is by invitation-only. We offer this exclusively for our best clients who are serious about getting great results in their business. This is a mastermind program to share ideas and implement changes.

Which option feels like the best fit for you at this time?

OUR MEMBER ENROLLMENT PROCESS

We assume that you have read our Cash Flow Playbook and are interested in joining our Cash Flow Club. You can download the Cash Flow Playbook here if you have not already read it:

The Cash Flow Playbook is the cornerstone of everything we do. Please do not go any further until you have reviewed the materials in the Playbook.

We have a simple three step process for Member Enrollment. We do this to ensure that we know with confidence that we can help you and to answer any questions that you might have before we agree to work together.

1. Clarity Worksheet - quick worksheet option for you and our team to determine if we should consider working together or not.
2. Strategy Worksheet - detailed analysis as to how we might work together. Our team reviews your responses to determine the next step.
3. Strategy Session - once we truly believe that we can assist you and your business, we review your Strategy Worksheet answers and give you guidance as to your next steps in the program.

We will contact you within 48 business hours of receiving your Strategy Worksheet responses to let you know next steps, If, based on your preliminary answers, we believe that we might be able to assist you with Cash Flow Club, we will onboard you and schedule a Strategy Session.

We use the more detailed answers that you provide on this Strategy Worksheet to determine exactly how we believe that we can help you. Based on your answers, we will either advise you that we can help you and how we plan to do so OR that we are not a fit to work together. Please do not be offended if we decide that working together is not a fit. It is not personal and it has everything to do with how our course is structured.

The first step after you join our program is to schedule a Strategy Session. We want to be 100% clear on your fit for our program. We invest in you and ask you to do the same with us. We want you to be successful right out of the gate.

CLARITY WORKSHEET

Take 10 to 15 minutes to complete our Clarity Worksheet. This is a quick option for you and our team to determine if we should consider working together or not. We will contact you within 48 hours of you completing our Clarity Worksheet to confirm next steps.

Complete our Clarity Worksheet here...

https://www.globalwellnesshq.com/worksheets/bkzTsFvmyUiMdtKrXp8dNFvP

STRATEGY WORKSHEET

Once we confirm that we believe we can help you, the second step is for you to spend 20 to 30 minutes completing our Strategy Worksheet. This is a detailed analysis as to how we might work together. Our team reviews your responses to determine the next step. We will contact you within 48 hours of you completing our Strategy Worksheet to confirm next steps.

Complete our Strategy Worksheet here...

https://www.globalwellnesshq.com/worksheets/WswWNMYjAJxtZNLrCdNjYinY

STRATEGY SESSION

Once we accept your membership application, we will send you details to confirm your enrolment. Once your enrolment is confirmed, we will also contact you to schedule your Strategy Session. You will meet with one of our Cash Flow Consultants to create a working plan for your business. Your Cash Flow Plan will be unique to you and will ensure that you have practical action steps right from our first interaction.

FREQUENTLY ASKED QUESTIONS

These are some of the questions people most frequently ask us:

Why did you create Cash Flow Club?
We are a group of entrepreneurs and business experts who are sick and tired of watching businesses struggle needlessly.

We created Cash Flow Club to share critical resources that mean the difference between merely surviving or thriving in business.

Why would I want to be part of Cash Flow Club?
A lot of entrepreneurs and business owners tell us that they are alone in their business. They can't talk to their spouses about challenges. They won't talk to employees about challenges. And, they definitely don't share their challenges with their suppliers.

We created Cash Flow Club to be a safe space for business leaders to find the resources they need to improve business cash flow.

We invite you to join Cash Flow Club if you would like to be part of a like-minded community that wants to build their businesses with intention.

I am not ready to commit to Cash Flow Club right now, when will you launch the next cohort?

We plan on launching a new cohort every quarter. The next cohort will likely launch on November 1, 2023. We cannot guarantee that we will have room for new members as we will give priority to business associates of existing members.

How do I receive an invitation to join the Elite Membership?
We only invite our best participants to join this group. It might sound elitist, but if you must ask to join, you are likely not ready to join.

We restrict membership deliberately. Our Elite Members are those who are serious about their business and are willing to do what it takes to thrive.

We do not want you to suffer in this group if you are not ready to commit to the work.

We will challenge you to take massive action, so join us only if you are serious about growth.

JOIN OUR EMAIL LIST

Do you want to receive monthly newsletter updates about Cash Flow Club? Join our email list and see what we do.

ARE YOU AN ACCOUNTING PROFESSIONAL?

We offer a special membership option for Accounting Professionals.

We created Cash Flow Club to help local business owners grow and scale their business.

We have created an exclusive community for accounting professionals who want to help their clients manage Cash Flow.

We recognize that you are smart enough to create your own programs and offerings. However, we also recognize that time is precious to you. We have created a full curriculum and program that you can offer to your clients.

https://www.globalwellnesshq.com/products/184780-Cash-Flow-Club-for-Accounting

CASH FLOW CLUB FOR ACCOUNTING PROFESSIONALS!

We created this Club to help local business owners grow and scale their business. We have created an exclusive community for accounting professionals who want to help their clients manage Cash Flow. We recognize that you are smart enough to create your own programs and offerings. However, we also recognize that time is precious to you. We have created a full curriculum and program that you can offer to your clients.

We recommend that you offer a three level program to your best clients. As they engage and get results, you can open your Cash Flow Club Program to more clients. When you follow our program, our goal is to help you generate at least $10,000 a month in new revenues in about 10 hours of time from existing clients. Once you have the basics in place, you can then grow by offering this to more of your existing clients and to new clients.

All our options below give you the tools that you need in order to start and run a profitable Cash Flow Club for existing and new clients.

We offer month to month options to smooth out your cash flow and to make sure that you are generating positive cash flow every month.

We offer four options for membership:

1. Month to Month Silver Membership: Our silver membership includes unlimited access to our weekly recorded trainings. We share at least one valuable lesson per week via recorded content. The focus will be on immediately actionable tips that you can leverage today to grow your accounting business. We will show you step by step how to build and grow your own Cash Flow Club. The silver membership level is our lowest cost option because you will be doing the steps with our guidance. Your price includes support and materials for up to ten clients.
2. Month to Month Gold Membership: Our gold membership includes everything in our silver membership. We include weekly live Q&A calls that are exclusively for our Gold Members. We will work with you to build and grow your own Cash Flow Club. Your price includes support and materials for up to twenty clients.

3. Month to Month Elite Membership: This is by invitation-only. We offer this exclusively for our best clients who are serious about getting great results by offering Cash Flow Club in their business. This is a mastermind program to share ideas and implement changes. We include a full concierge service where our dedicated team will prepare everything that you need and help you manage your Cash Flow Club. Your price includes support and materials for up to fifty clients.

4. Annual Prepaid Elite Membership: This is by invitation-only. This includes everything in the month to month elite membership, with a few valuable bonuses added in. Our annual prepaid elite members will receive quarterly strategy sessions and access to a part-time virtual assistant to manage the day to day operations of your Cash Flow Club.

Which option feels like the best fit for you at this time?

NOTES

PART 9: SPONSORING CASH FLOW CLUB PLAYBOOK

NOTES

We created the Cash Flow Club Playbook to share resources with our community. Our Playbook is a physical book (published on Amazon) and a digital publication that is readily available (and free) for our audience.

Cash Flow Club is a publication showcasing cash flow tips, tactics, and strategies for businesses of all sizes. We will feature experts who contribute to the success of businesses. Our audience is entrepreneurs, business owners, and organization leaders who are serious about the success of their business.

We are able to distribute Cash Flow Club only through the support of our sponsors. We would love to feature your business in our publication if it serves you.

ADVERTISING RATES*

Front Cover Package - $3,150.00
- Front cover, full color picture or montage Credit on the contents page
- Full page advertisement Full page of editorial
- Hyperlink from the editorial in the digital version to any dedicated URL
- Listing in the business directory

Special Position - $2,525.00
- One of inside front cover, inside back cover, or back cover
- Full page advertisement Full page of editorial
- Hyperlink from the editorial in the digital version to any dedicated URL
- Listing in the business directory

Full Page Advertisement - $1,925.00
- Hyperlink from the editorial in the digital version to any dedicated URL
- Listing in the business directory

Half Page Advertisement - $1,075.00
- Hyperlink from the editorial in the digital version to any dedicated URL
- Listing in the business directory

Quarter Page Advertisement - $750.00
- Hyperlink from the editorial in the digital version to any dedicated URL
- Listing in the business directory

All advertisements are in full color.

*All prices are before applicable taxes and are current as of August 16, 2023.

ACTIVE MILITARY, VETERANS, AND MILITARY SPOUSES

We honor you on Veteran's Day and every day.

At Global Wellness HQ, we recognize that the average citizen would not be free to pursue their own personal wellness journeys if not for the sacrifices of our active military, veterans, and military spouses. We believe that we owe each and every one of you a massive debt of gratitude. "Thank you for your service" is our first act of gratitude. Though, it is heart-felt, it is not enough.

We fully support our military families. We will highlight resources specifically to assist our military families. However, to put our money where our hearts are, we also offer free advertising to any military-owned business. We mean it when we say "thank you." Your money is no good with us, you have already paid in service. Reach out to https://www.linkedin.com/in/jeff-borschowa for more details.

ADVERTISEMENT TECHNICAL SPECIFICATIONS

Full Page Trim size: 210mm wide x 297mm high Type area: 180mm wide x 267mm high Bleed area: 215mm x 302mm high

Half Page Horizontal Trim size: 210mm wide x 148mm high Type area: 195mm wide x 129mm high Bleed area: 215mm x 153mm high

Half Page Vertical Trim size: 105mm wide x 297mm high Type area: 93mm wide x 282mm high Bleed area: 110mm x 302mm high

Quarter Page Trim size: 99.5mm wide x 140mm high Type area: 95mm wide x 135mm high Bleed area: 105mm x 145mm high

Quotations are available if you do not have material but would like to advertise. We can help you design your advertisement.

Learn more about advertising with us by visiting:

https://www.globalwellnesshq.com/cash-flow-club

NOTES

NOTES

PART 10: CASH FLOW RESOURCES

NOTES

We are just building out this section of the book. Check LinkedIn as we will be posting updates.

Our intention is to do the research and share our findings so that you don't have to.

We will be sharing books, podcasts, courses, software, and other resources that you can use as a starting point for your own personal cash flow journey of discovery.

Some of our favorite resources include:

- Online financial management software, such as Sage Business Cloud, Xero or QuickBooks Online - you can't prepare and monitor results if you do not have accurate and timely accounting records. Online software allows for real-time business data if used properly.
- Cash flow forecasting software, such as Dryrun, My Cash Flow Story, Float, Reach Reporting, etc. - if you have a more complicated business, you may need a more complicated Business Budget or forecast.
- Business reporting tools, like Tally Street, Chata.ai, Fathom, Clarity, Reach Reporting, etc. These tools can give you very precise insight into your business, allowing you to make business decisions in real time. Your trusted advisors should be able to help you choose and implement the best tools for your business.
- Mastering Cash Flow for Business Owners: Adopt Key Cash Flow Optimization Strategies and You Will NEVER Have a Sleepless Night Again! by Craig Alexander Rattray
- Financial Foreplay: Whip Your Business into Shape - Take Home More Cash by Rhondalynn Korolak
- Pandemic Cash Flow: Cash flow issues kill nearly 30% of businesses. Why it happens, and how to prevent it by Blaine Bertsch
- Profit First: Transform Your Business from a Cash-Eating Monster to a Money-Making Machine by Mike Michalowicz
- Traction: Get a Grip on Your Business by Gino Wickman
- The Automatic Customer: Creating a Subscription Business in Any Industry by John Warrillow
- Talk Like TED: The 9 Public-Speaking Secrets of the World's Top Minds by Carmine Gallo
- TED TALKS: The Official TED Guide to Public Speaking by Chris J. Anderson
- Presentation Zen: Simple Ideas on Presentation Design and Delivery by Garr Reynolds
- Expert Secrets: The Underground Playbook for Creating a Mass Movement of People Who Will Pay for Your Advice by Russel Brunson
- Retention Point: The Single Biggest Secret to Membership and Subscription Growth for Associations, SAAS, Publishers, Digital Access, Subscription Boxes and all Membership and Subscription-Based Businesses by Robert Skrob
- The Ultimate Sales Machine: Turbocharge Your Business with Relentless Focus on 12 Key Strategies by Chet Holmes
- The E-Myth Revisited: Why Most Small Businesses Don't Work and What to Do About It by Michael E. Gerber

- E-Myth Mastery: The Seven Essential Disciplines for Building a World-Class Company by Michael E. Gerber
- SYSTEMology: Create time, reduce errors, and scale your profits with proven business systems by David Jenyns and Michael E. Gerber
- 80/20 Sales and Marketing: The Definitive Guide to Working Less and Making More by Perry Marshall
- Detox, Declutter, Dominate: How to Excel by Elimination by Perry Marshall and Robert Skrob
- The Slight Edge: Secret to a Successful Life by Jeff Olson
- Getting to Yes: Negotiating Agreement Without Giving In by Roger Fisher, William Ury, et al.
- Never Split the Difference: Negotiating as If Your Life Depended On It by Tahl Raz
- Instant Influence: How to Get Anyone to Do Anything--Fast by Michael Pantalon
- Influence: The Psychology of Persuasion by Robert B. Cialdini

What are your favorite cash flow resources?

ABOUT JEFF BORSCHOWA

Jeff is an entrepreneur, author, educator, and coach for business owners looking to grow their business to the next level. Throughout his 33 years in the fields of business, accounting, and coaching, Jeff's innovative approach to Client Getting has consistently surpassed the expectations of his clients in a broad range of industries.

Jeff's expertise has led him to be a guest speaker for many respected organizations in the accounting industry. To date, Jeff has helped hundreds of business owners find their own path to Client Getting.

Jeff created Clientology™ to guide business owners towards implementing effective Client Getting strategies in their own business. In 2022, Jeff launched a new and updated Clientology™ Growth System to directly address the unique challenges business owners faced due to COVID-19. The Clientology™ Growth System is based on Jeff's proven formula and decades of experience. The Clientology™ Growth System is ideal for local business experts who are looking to increase their freedom, money, and impact in their business.

JOIN CASH FLOW CLUB

We share strategies and practical tips that business owners and entrepreneurs can implement immediately to improve the overall cash flow in their business.

We will talk about inbound cash flow, outbound cash flow, and managing cash flows overall.

Our primary focus is to generate additional revenues and reduce overall expenses, leaving more cash in your business to fund your life goals.

We share the advice that our top experts have field tested over decades as advisors to large and small businesses (and everything in between). Put our collective wisdom to work in your business today!

Scan the QR Code or go directly to our website here:

https://www.globalwellnesshq.com/cash-flow-club

www.ingramcontent.com/pod-product-compliance
Lightning Source LLC
Chambersburg PA
CBHW080916260726
48661CB00009B/3692